# Breathing with Wings in October Light

Thomas Cox

IGLOO
PRESS

San Francisco, CA

Igloo Press, Tucson, Arizona
www.igloopress.net

ISBN 978-0-9787608-9-2

For information, write:
Igloo Press
2940 16th St. Suite 216,
San Francisco, CA 94103

*FOR THE DAKINI IN US ALL*

# CONTENTS

## I.

## II.

*FOR THE DAKINI IN US ALL*

# CONTENTS

## I.

## II.

# III.

# IV.

I

# October Rain

1.

A swarm of seagulls in the mountains transfixes
the poet in his reverie to find along a desert road

star-maps imprinted in cholla's barbed designs.
October has broken into fissionable clouds,

hoof-marks in porcelain-blue, a visual elixir
to stain the foxhole happiness of his mind.

What doesn't dry up in its divinity after a good rain?
Light itself sings to the sparrow of its madness

from a treetop, green pine needles growing ever-
green in their lancing upward, bark wrinkling

in their wake, a litheness in the way light caresses
the depths of its folds, another Monday here.


2.

Shall he eat the sweetmeat of his love for her
this morning?  The poet is just a man, a dark horse,

old equus burning coal, tawny neck arching up,
a train rumbling out of a mountain like a hearse,

wheels molten, with spokes reddening into a blur,
windows flashing by filled with clouds like drapes

at the exact hour of midnight, rails colliding
at the midpoints of constellations, all diameter

blown apart in the sudden rain.  Does he know
what love is?  Will this road bank back to that side

of his knowledge which brays?  Does it matter?
He arrives home.  What he doesn't know goes.


3.


A hosannah of wetness! A woman's navel
filling with rain.  No breaking through a mountain's

brooding cliffs after this, there's too much valley
to be mapped out while the poet's eyes darken into jade.

Sitting down to breakfast of melon,
his gaze contains the kitchen window, oleander

spreading its leaves into a soft rain's haze.
His chair is made of wood, his table blue ceramic.

Outside, no wind to countenance, nor cumuli
to sketch into his mind, everything gone but this stucco

wall surrounding his yard, bracketing his phrase,
and blood, yes, and love, love to quicken his eye.

## Facing It

October turns to March,
my loneliness, my love.

Today's going to scorch
me by the look of

the dawn's ochre-red
blossoming over Babo-

quivari, from my bed
facing it in the cabin

of my Ford Explorer,
waking up to loneliness

and no barriers
in a raven's exacting prowess.

Such loneliness to flood
every expanse!  I'd dreamt

I'd returned to my boyhood,
unable to preempt

its foolish extravagance —
days of marigold

and cattails and wooden fences
and snowdrifts yet unscaled,

somehow unable to find
any landmark once visited —

and now, awake again, I stand
in water, grinning and naked,

whooping at the freshness
of the air, alive to its scope

running everywhere to kiss
me right on the lips.

When the sun flares
wide over the mountain

the way sage flowers
into the heart of this pain,

into ordinary transcendence,
the depthless sky above,

it resumes its hydrogen trance,
lets go of ordinary love,

O my Beloved caught in the rain
brightening the first

crimson blooms of ocotillo, stain
on my gathering thirst!

# A Red Dog Called Mars

I've lost the arc of each ankle-bone
in a red eye, a pair of crutches
still leaning against an open doorway,

beyond which fields of dandelion trace
the outline of a sun in a dark room.
A canary whistles in an unseen corner.

No gangrene—the violet threads
of capillaries branch
away from desiccated skin,

a scar encircling
each ankle, both feet
once severed, now anchored again, a little numb

at the hem,
an odor of burnt mesquite
at the fossil-ends of soles, in spiderweb stitches.

Where once these feet traveled, their imprint
in water still reflecting
winter-gray,

standing up now seems akin
to dancing with pygmies, or
striding with giants down a creekbed

to marble monuments
flecked with remnants of butterfly wings.
Up above:  old planet Mars,

that loping red dog,
that hammer and anvil,
that fusion driving

the flower back into its seed,
wherein there is no standing up —
only looking

up a mountain burning with aspen,
this fire like blood in rock,
this smoke opening into petals,

this desire to walk
the arches of these feet
God's shadow breathing in the heat

of Mars, ember burning at my navel.
Old planet, more than blood,
you cradle this sickle moon.

## Behind the Catalinas

In a creek under cottonwoods, watercress
leaps into my hand, bittersweet fronds
I take into my mouth like silverfish,
striated gills and long hair pooled

on the water's surface, here, at a closed down
boy's camp, an afternoon turning to thickets
of veins, rusting bedframes, a wooden bridge
sturdy as a mainsail.  Then a walk down

an abandoned road, a woman and a child
at my side, an image cut into watery glass,
sliding off the cool air against our faces,
each step a beckoning into distances

unknowably filled with caresses, articulations,
diameters of watercress and twin cottonwoods joined
at their bases, a bench between them.
We sit there in the sunlight for a while,

heads tilted up in opposite directions,
over a bed of moldering cottonwood leaves —
such quietude leads to happiness
like a door not to be opened

anywhere but in this act of walking, this curve
of hip and pelvis steadied by a spine
and descending a hill, before turning back
at dusk, barely silhouettes

against an evening of decaying dormitories,
no footfall behind us but in sparks
of fading sunlight, no ghost at all to become us
now, twilight shading your shoulders.

## October Light

1.

leans through 5 O'clock sky to settle
against her face, as I lean back
against the remains of an old mortar wall,
a wheel perhaps once from a stagecoach
to my left, as she takes
this light with her camera,

its eclipse hushing the fragrance of the orange tree
overhead, enclosing the pecans in perpetuity,

shaping her in the moment she kneels down
beside me…Ah, there I am on a digital screen,
smiling at her.

That night, a dream
wakes me, her hand woven into mine in October light.

At the end of the night,
in her Nissan wagon,
a lifetime of pain gives way to space

unbounded, to be held by a camera's
fade into memory, her wide arms
for a lengthening moment.

2.

Her daughter, Kya Rose,
whose mimicking of alligators and moose
between movies delights
even the velvet rope she pole-
vaults over, in a game
of tag in a theatre corridor,

now sleeps in her mother's lap, dreaming before
the end, when the kid gets
his rightful inheritance
from Duvall and Caine
in *Secondhand Lions*.

Ah, the sweet fade
of Arabia, Texas, diminutively made
to seem quaint,
while the night outside drifts into vastness,
stars unraveling into eyes.


3.

During the ride home,
I tell her my brother is gone,
father too, and daughter sent
to Minnesota on the back
of her mother, as though none of them
had ever been, as she holds
fast to the steering wheel.

She pulls up to my curb, my red brick.

What comes
of a steel gate, a copper fountain the shape of agave, a hole
in the ground where a pond will soon be?
What fish will I be enraptured by?

Will they too dream of water lilies rising
to weave themselves into canopies
shading lotus in summertime?

What remains
when the soil itself seems
to run through my hands
faster than a mirror's quicksilver

when I kneel down
and drop a totem pole cactus into the ground?

What vanishes breathes again,
doesn't it?  And what comes

of a dream in the morning, waking up
to a voice, an echo, a breathable silence
binding words of her daughter

to the sound of water
outside my door, sleep
cascading away with the force of a vow:
Yes, her words.  *Your paths are together now.*

# November Cold

1.

This hibiscus blossom, a flaring
orange to rival electrical storms,
pours out

its nebula
into the finest strands
of rain

one afternoon.

What it touches is the passing
ghost of the world
in your hands.

2.

Datura turns to winter
before its sacred blossoming,
the ground wet

with a dragon's breath,
a thrush's outcry embedded
in the deep oriental blue of October.

The way you once arrived
at my shoulder
is how snow rides
the horizon's mountains.

3.

The sun burns off
glaze of dew.

The spirit of one's Father banks
on the involutions
of what evaporates —

and there you are,
coral
and saguaro seed,

breast and heavenly sky,
loam, cactus spine,
poem's rind! — edge

of my mind's
drifting arc

toward olive-flesh,
apple-pit,
this dissolving

ache of death
into unvarnished sunlight
tracing stone.

Who gets up
in the morning —
who touches

the cold unremembering
ash at the heart of fire?

# II

# Cello Sonata in A Minor

*A recital performed by Nancy Green with Venerable
Ontul Rinpoché in attendance*

Cheekbone and eyelash and braid
at her back, a cello cradled

with a doppelganger's insouciant aplomb,
who could deny such thrum

and verve, as though each stroke
of bow beheld a lightning's streak

reflected in a mirror, a ghost's mirage
of music inlaid in notes that age

this marrow into youthfulness,
a springtime of Brahms, lithe

as a monsoon climbing mountain-ladders.
Flesh becomes flesh, scales scattering

the noise of thought.  (What 'i' is left
to witness another full moon's drift?)

Across the room, a vajra master
listens entirely, imperturbably, vast

in his silent measuring of notes
breaking across eye, heart, throat.

The parlor walls fade into light
for a moment, and Hayagriva brightly

blazes from the moon-disc throne
of his mandala, horse's-head thrown

back to weigh this barest of
fluctuations, this cascading wave

of string upon string, of mirth
and melody wedded to lessen the wrath

in his stance.  He absorbs the fire
all around him, his consort Vajra-

varahi spinning around to see
what it is that might ease

her beloved's dragon-roar and stamp.
Then the walls dissolve back, clamp

into place; a hush radiates
from dust, bookshelves, air-grates;

*this is it, relax into alertness!*
*unbind yourself into unbroken bliss!*

## Shunyata

*For Tiko*

1.

Ineluctable marrow, sinking
into breath, lazing
about:

how "The Girl from Ipanema"
softens
your face
before you speak of friendship,

and I, I
unable to write
anything but

haiku treatises on how light
breaks
across your skin,

revel in Joao
Gilberto's silk-inflection:
what are we if not

the who of a blazing into marrow,
and so I let go

into a mirror's
flashing into emptiness,

2.

and face the Wall
of Mind:

it hovers close to the sun:
sings of union with every
juniper pine, jagged

acacia, dreaming mushroom:
embraces a
sharp reflection

and cutting arc
across your diamond-complexion:


3.


wherefore personal pronouns
are irrelevant:

all praise diminishes
into universal radiance:

globe mallow by the roadside
are like a mountain's petticoats:

breath against mirror so steep
when seeing myself

in the shape of you
having just left

after a dinner of tuna
and talk of love:


4.


the way a daughter
holds her head above water,

observes a strip
of cumulus straight up

above, a few bats
divebombing palm to pivot

in air as though it were
a portal into *here* as it becomes *there:*

how she states, her eyes the light
of lilies, how beautiful

it is, the wonder like bread
pounded out of seed:

how, like a bird
in snow, vapor curds

itself above, dissolves
into halves,

its looms a hundred wings
beating

back upon themselves,
in wave after wave,

a wild iris turning violet
in direct sunlight,

and so the recipe says
then turn away,

eat the spare bones
boiled down

at midday,
because they are who you say

you are, rapt emblems
that once came

to twine themselves around us
baskets of wildflowers:

5.

leave the light behind
stay the orange rind

huddle in flowering mist
stray from grist

because it will all well
up again a tidal swell

a bubbling vat
of alleycats

a troubling gruel
of angels born fools:


6.

then a swift blossoming into god
derives us, impedes

luminescence in giving way
to who becomes the Month of May —


7.

in this absence of fire
at my finger-

tips all asway
this month of May

in its circumferences,
dizzying fences:

8.

a great white bird broadly circles
overhead, drops down with the gait
of a tern, lands with a softness
of jaguar feet, dances

right up, and puts her head
and beak under my arm:

in her eyes
rainbows:  in her beak rows
of baby teeth:

laughter in the tilt of her neck:
wisdom in her feathered bemused look:
sorrow in the cant of her head to
and fro:

in all of it
flight to reckon
with the sleep of stars: vast distillating points
that reach out

to helios, compost, the grayness between
dry riverbeds and signposts, rusting bridges and the slopes
they mean to connect:

and oh! the pain
of wings rustling
near ribs grown suddenly hollow
with sunlight:

the updraft
of her departure
entering fingertips:

a wind sweeping to fill
every tundra, plateau, peak, arroyo:

before I can begin to ask why
oh why has this bird
of waterways come
to this desert place.

# Snapshots of a Father Dying on a Hospital Gurney

1.

Christ, the terrible wrenching
birth must have entailed!


2.

I sat
on the crown of a cardinal's forehead and
couldn't grasp the precise enormity
of the *who* who was the *who* to hook
flesh to cranial bone, so I craned
for a better look at the shadow swirling
into sunlight, thinking I might actually
come to know what melancholy brightness
shimmered at my wrists and palms:

his body alone lay there, nostrils
caving in — and a female priest, so
evangelical

in the hospital light, glared
at me when I pulled out
my bag of blessed sand,
a few grains for his fontanel,
magnets to help

eject out his crown
evanescent spark of heart-mind, a sudden cannon's
expulsion into a lotus flower

tinged with blue and aching
to open my shaking hands:

3.

for this I that looked into i foresaw
leaves lingering in mounds,  all the
worms of a very small plot of ground deciding
they'd had enough and vanishing
into that nitrogen between seeds and their blossoms

and the years floating by on a swallow's wings:

one lung completely shut down,
the other dwindling down
a machine's graph:


4.

i've drunk the sweet radiance
on the surface of all things green
by the time I settle down
to iridescent necks
of pigeons taking a drink
from waterfall and wind
in my chimes:

to set all of heaven to recruit
hell in service
to you-
deity, i-
deity, bird-

deity
of all species of bird lining up on a telephone line in an
alphabet
only wind can decipher,

when all dreams float away
in the witnessing,
the entropy:

5.

whereas the looking could no longer
look at itself and there was
no more waiting to stop
an opening into a crevasse's

depth, where i
sat playing solitaire all night and

the sun blinked its ace
of spades right
into my face,

as i rose
to sweetly touch the very tiniest gongs hanging
in midair, as my hands shook
to touch his crown,
even so—

how space itself floats
inside the very thing you think is going
to land on your head but instead
circles gravity to push its cape

over your shoulders, with no harness to hitch
yourself to, only the swinging
of a prayer wheel keeping
the pull of things together.

# Internal Spontaneous Combustion

There a sparrow's
shadow above my shrine,
hopping across air

like nothing at all, to break
away, be
blind for half

a moment, then
a whole.  Likenesses
dovetail into sameness

like water…no,
water itself:  a breathing
barrel of it hanging

above flute duodenum,
tuba appendix,
oboe spleen,

heart conductor
raising a baton
to ruin every notion of air —

only feathers
left to drive
this world bound

to epidermis
and shape and Don Quijote
and what burns

so visibly at the base
of the nape, a ring
of fire, a cold flame,

a quiet,
evacuating space,
this moment's blind grace.

## Seventeen Ways of Looking at the Journey to the Inner Beloved

1

no markers to be found
in grey-green water growing warm
with sunlight—

2

sweat of rosemary
blanketing
an indissoluble oxygen—

3

what sky levitates
in your palm cupping
springwater for Kya Rose—

4

what vanishing havens
these molecules are to be dropped
into sky—

5

cucumbers and watermelon burst
out of soil the way
water breathes—

6

a walk down the street beckons
in midjune with moisture
of trumpet vine —


7

as for returns the light
of October gathers
immense waterways —


8

what floats at eye-level
is leaf caught in the firmament
of water —


9

a touch of crimson lingers
in the half-light of a moon
rippling


10

with seed drowning
in a river composed not of
water but of breath —


11

no water at noon to fill
a teacup in sweltering
arroyos —

12

cloud bleaches adobe
to the color of eggshell
and rainwater —


13

a sparrow falls into a pond
to be lifted out
with a glass plate —


14

out of the moon a mass of hair
bids deft hands to touch
wet surfaces —


15

sleep glazes the water
of the world pooling
in a red ant's wide eye —


16

pine stump as perch
for a hundred species
of bird and a pair of heads —


17

sun goes down
to anchor mesquite saplings
in hedgerows of dying fern —

# After Hotel Rwanda

1.

So I wonder, in this harsh light,
in the whiff of your breath, in the grass
heaping at your belly, in the abdomen
of the cricket, the dream
of your crown,

what determines
plot and all its attendant assassinations
at the heart
of simply wanting to write a love poem?

In answer,
grass is bled dry by the wind, acacia
upends

its thorns,

a heat unlike
any pain
boils out of my flesh:

think *cool*, think
*now's the time to start*

*what I don't know,*
aphrodisiacs
maybe,

starry-eyed anemones, lava flows like
fords, curtains, laurel wreathes.

2.

*Light secures
us all,* whispers

the blue heron, a trout
sliding

down its throat.
A gravity of afternoon

weighs the devout
bay at my fingertips.

Duende brews the best
coffee, its bitter

grounds the blessing
of us all,

light of marigold
stamen, of water shining

with primordial grief,
sandstone, trees.


3.


Now simply
to wake up, Lorca!  Trace
sinew, follow

light
away from its source, gauge
its diameter, without

spiders and their
angling creep,
empty facets

in how starlight now glazes
the growth of pears,
the spinning years.


4.

Maybe tomorrow I'll drive off
into a sunset made of pure agate.
Maybe it'll rain and no
restitution will be found
in its silent pattering,

its temple ground
getting lighter every day, shining with starlight.
Maybe sleep will come

to Africa
and we'll all stroll backward
through the remainder of our years.
Maybe there'll be no more maybes.
Maybe a grain of sand

in the palm of my hand
will begin to weigh
with the tides, whisper
surf, gravity, moon's heart.

Maybe a rose will no longer resemble a rose.
Maybe traffic will part one day
at Campbell and Grant and a
thoroughbred racehorse from Arabia

will go galloping past.
Maybe the price of tea will determine
what the revolution will look like again.
Maybe nobody will come to their own funeral.

5.

Grass, velvet
spear, grazing
note, risen
froth, elbowing

stone:  meditate
in sea-water,
watch thoughts
gain salt, bread, luminosity

in the simplest hours spent
listening to water
pull itself apart
into a sacred geometry,

a poem
smelling of freshly ground corn,
a walk to the park.
In my dream I'm mute and deaf.
It fills with red ants spiraling

into eights, scattering
twigs, and I wake and the world
is quiet for a moment,
driverless but for one

keening sound —
the passage of light
like hands pushing
into water's open rooms.

# A 'Riwo Sang Chod' Fire Puja at Konchog Nyida Ling

*For Choejor Rinpoché*

Sunset comes pouring
over the hills
before Nirvana
derives itself from
the grit of my nails,

route 87 from here
to Showlow snaking
in u-turns down
canyon embankments, the back-
alley of my throat

swollen with a virus,
the third incarnation
of Choejor Rinpoché
seeming to doze beside me
in the passenger seat,

implacable while drops
of stomach medicine eat their way
into his retina — oops!
Off to Showlow Medical Center's
waiting room, where this Mormon

Native American guy
in blue jeans, a Styrofoam
cup in hand and steeped
in a cloud of alcohol, asks,
"What are you doing?"

"Counting mantra," I say,
my mala beads slipping
through my fingers with each
Guru Rinpoché seven-line prayer
as he sits back in his chair,

bristling for a fight, then
leans over to his friend
whose mother or daughter or wife —
hard to say — is in ICU,
maybe brain-damaged,

to say, man, he's really sorry…
At this juncture best not to mention
we're on our way
to Konchog Nyida Ling, meaning
"the center where the Three Jewels are practiced

under the light of the sun and moon"
to perform a fire ceremony that feeds
hungry ghosts and demons the smoke
of juniper, yogurt, white flour, incense, cookies,
butter, rice, prayer flags.

A little later, on his way out, swaying
back on his heels before being swallowed
by the sliding door entrance, he proclaims,
"Jesus is the only way to salvation,
and *I* can discuss *that* with *you*…"

Choejor Rinpoche, one of whose previous incarnations
is depicted in the Drikung
Kagyu refuge tree, lightly takes
hold of my arm
and whispers, "What *are*

you doing?"  Well, what arrival
then that next day to hills
of juniper and sage and a pair
of trailers, one derelict and mouse-
ridden, the other intact, ready

for retreatants, and what
to say of this yogi, beaming
in shade as he incants
this smoke to liberate
those caught between here and

there, light and darkness,
dream and decaying metal?
These days are winding down
to embers and a gathering storm
of prayers to encircle

the globe, fill in
ozone, heap the plates
of starving refugees with the finest
molé, eradicate
depleted uranium

munitions from the minefields
of Iraq, bring back
the marches of MLK and sandal-
footed Gandhi, peaceniks
and stubble-headed

monks burning up!  O Rinpoché!  There,
in your sunglasses hiding eyes still
bright fields of lava, I can only say
there is nothing of the three times
I won't do for you.

# III

# At Haru's in Manhattan

*For Adi, after her brother's suicide*


Across what distance might a leaf's
vein enshadow
a space between eyes,

a melting radiance
in the looking glass
of the restaurant's window

onto pedestrians
bolting down side streets
away from loss,

into alleyways hidden
from such a place,
as though they strode

toward some peripheral garden
of gardenias,
fizzling snapdragons,

where death had no weight
in the silver dimes in the bowls
of beggars wanting only

solace, restitution, dreams.
You spoke of Israel's
desert, of breaking bread

with Bedouins.
The light of the afternoon
curled around your eyes,

as rounds of salmon
sushi disappeared
into air, breath, fire.

What loss is not taken
from us in that hour
of exaltation

and happiness?
Afterward, a crowded thoroughfare,
a subway stricken with graffiti,

a journey back to another
kind of desert.
I bow to this hour

every day, just as I now
bow to you, Adi, grieving
dreamer, fire-bearer.

## Breathing with Wings

1.

Is there someone
beside me
in my garden this morning?

I've just planted an evening primrose, loam
in mounds at my feet, a forest mulch,
when I hear wings

slipping past,
coming to rest
between brick and begonia,
strutted with light —

upon which an angel on his back rises
out of the froth of a storm, vacant

hazel eyes reflecting back
a ceaseless swaying
of firmament-cloud,
drawn star-blinds,

to witness these
sunflowers opening
to earth's memory

of risen stone,
not at all

resting in this beauty
of desert willow blossoms'
pink effulgence.

**2.**

What happens when each wing
grazes an updraft's downward-curving

blade?  Does air
itself resume

its breathless space
and longitude? —

what vacuum might replace
these steel wings

when, in late afternoon, I pull up a withered
zinnia, a flock
of seven sparrows huddled
together in desert willow suddenly
bursting into conversation —

a matter of the greatest gossip?
Such flurry of wings
the air will never be the same.


**3.**

Breathing with wings,
I settle into bone, drifting
away from cloud-light
enveloping sky.

I dig another hole.

Such wings are the very air
surrounding us all

in how they lift this sapling mesquite
slowly out of earth, ruffle

the neighbor's palm-fronds,
embrace the towering eucalyptus
across the street.

Red carnatians go into earth.

*Is there no boundary to looking?*

Are there no palms to plumb
for their lines' inquisitions?

Will we layer ourselves
in memory bound
by an angel's wings?

*What would happen to wind without gravity?*

Might it touch
your wings'
engraving ascent,

shape
the arc of your hands
reaching up
to put the rain back

before gently laying you back down?

# God Never Gave It in the First Place

This thin fiftyish blonde with her petite dog—
salt and pepper fur—steps down
the wooden stairs through giant cedar

just behind me
to say:

"There are two things that bring
a woman up against reality.
Buying a house or a bathing-suit."

The long perspective faded skin brings
stretches out

the length of this beach paradise
at South Whidbey State Park

to a series of wide doors
closing one behind the next,
each an empty
crab-shell

offering up
the blistering skin of Admiralty Inlet,
somewhere between
the Pacific and Mulkiteo Ferry.

I've been waiting for
this molting curl
of waves around
battered kelp, the knees
of this woman—

"Fighting the blues," she says.
"This is just what I needed."

My eyes rowing out
to the other shore, I say,
"Sink into them. They're your
pillow stuffed with the feathers
of the sandpiper."


*


Where memory goes:
A piece of driftwood
a boy throws onto a wave
at San Pablo Bay,

nearby an abandoned Chinese settlement,
a rusting pier and fishing-boat replica
called the "Grace Quan."

Now a few yachts bob
on petroleum waves,
here a family of five,
the father strutting down sand

to gather up his flock,
the mother calling
to the oldest boy

it's time to eat,
the youngest crawling across
a picnic table to his mother's arms
like a crab to the deepest

culvert of his shell,
their one daughter
quietly eating.

Memory pins itself to the map
of their swift departure
back to a Golden Gate

gridlock, an earthquake
of years.

\*

I row a boat
out between my years,
the one with an infant fist

running through it and the other
ducking behind a redwood canopy's
reflection in a waxing moon.

How did I come to this place
in the shade, so full
of knots in my veins?

I arrive at the other shore,
a city's spires
braced against the firmament of an ocean,

my eyes fastening themselves
to what blurs between
evanescence and motion

of fig-leaf so full
of sunlight lifting
and dissolving, lifting
and dissolving

no recompense can be made
between what can be
weighed and

what is.

# The Road through the Bitterroot Mountains

How many years have I desired
desire itself, this word that rings
with rivers fired
by song?

Stepping through my gate engraved
with the Tibetan syllable *Hung*,
bearing watercolor poems, she wavers
between flagstone and air, lungs

filling with a fragrance
of white persimmon tea...
Later, she's been replaced
by a river, this "she"

once arisen out of incense,
a dark blue of India,
and now the Clearwater in the Bitterroot Mountains
of Idaho,

and before that the slapping tail of a sea otter
off Whidbey Island
north of Seattle.
Her hair is wild,

with a touch of auburn and a hint
of white...Later, a beach
calls me to look more closely, almost squint,
into the ridges of clam-shells cinched

together, the salt-
wings of some fallen angel
still
adjoined,

while a purplish mass
of dead jellyfish billows
in surf like glass,
rubber and slime at once

when I take a stick to it,
the fog over the cove a footprint
in air.  An era flits
by, the rain grows faint

against a windshield,
and a winding road ends
with the word Beloved,
suave, impressionable, genderless.

*


I rest along the bank of a river,
more a creek, really, given its narrow
traverse past Lolo Hot Springs' one tavern,
a gift shop and museum full of arrows

of the Nez Perce, a hot bath-
house, a lodge and cabins,
its width
dividing me from the lens

of what I know and the image
not to be known.  I want to say
*here, this is knowledge,*
this drifting passage

of water; hold each palmful
fragment with tenderest
gratitude, step across its spilling
current to find a little rest.

In this the sound of Beloved,
play of afternoon light along its contour
a bell cocooned in its rapid.
In effect, this softening of glacial rock into future

cliff-faces is this wish to write
about a river, really only
to layer you into its strata,
to be free, finally —

\*

An immediate Gibraltar
in the firm anchoring of yellow grass
along the other shore.
I drink my wine, a shiraz

from Southeastern Australia,
balancing my glass' stem
against cedar-grain.  The flaw
in it all, my friend,

resounds within concavities
in an autumnal
freeze,
the crawl

of these shortening stanzas.
Where's the hastening end
now?  What hidden bonanzas
in the reeds

even an egret could pry loose
when I'm drunk
with what arcs, obtuse
layerings into a riverbank

of thistle pods, parabolas
of current, meandering bees,
a whispering grace
beyond peripheries,

dusk giving way to a moth's citadel of stars?
(Whatever trip you take, don't plan it.)
*Om Tare*.  Purple bloom of asters
nicks the edge of granite.

## Bivouacking into West Cochise Stronghold

A pair of deer
dart down this trail
once a native's foot path, their white tails

flashing at midmorning, a last fair
breath of summer on a November wind
at my back, an ancient Apache spirit-mind

quiet in its root's depth of alligator juniper.
I give way to a steep wash,
a boulder-effacement, the sash

of a native's rock house, where the stains
of war party fires still linger
in its granite ceiling,

where one can imagine
buffalo hide hung from the entrance
of a wickiup, the stance

of a scout just returned with news
of an advancing cavalry.
Its cool interior breathes

into my blood a shade
that leaps from rock to rock, a weave
across spruce, agave,

manzanita, all of light pooling
at the center of its blackest cave,
in their hard flint knives.

What dream carved into these walls
lifting and falling like water
under my hands, aflutter

with a butterfly's digressions?
I leap down boulders, as light
as silt in their crevices, a heightening

of nerve-endings with each
tenuous lunge forward
toward

a campfire of manzanita and spruce,
a greenish hue of mountainous rock
throwing its shadow, its dark

cape, across my shoulders.
So narrow and canopied this path!
Its deer's width

bridles my descent,
my arrival without arrival,
circumference, navel.

The haunt of the day
sharpens agave thorns,
sweet lavender shade born

out of the cast
of sunlight against
alligator bark, as though tensed

to strike.  To believe
beauty is in what vanishes
is to not relish

gravity too much.
It grazes on moonlight.
It hastens to ignite

shadow's underbelly,
its ash a helix-
shaped prefix

to an earth underneath,
a door leading nowhere—
no descent, no stair—

only the footprints
of a deer and a doe,
chaste with Autumn, incognito,

pulling the sun back
to its anchoring hold
on emptiness' prevaricating mold,

the shape of a woman
springing out of rock,
out of a deer's tracks,

a sunlight's lingering ebb
on her neck as we descend,
each bend's

latitude filling a stronghold,
carrying the weight
of her disappearing gait.

She is light itself,
risen up from the ground.
She is why the deer bounds.

# October Light Returns

1.

and November breaks into sodden
leaves under a kitchen window.


2.

A creek outside Bozeman, Montana brings up bellyfuls
of trout, a hook
piercing

limber pine, a drifting
afterglow of trellises
entering

stone, a leaping over
cowpies in the afternoon altering
the thin reeds

waking out of a pond,
a refrain of cattle in the hills,
a tasting of spring water in August

with eyes, truant
moon cupping silverfish
with palms like canyons,

as moose saunter up
like houses in the great icy gloom
of the Grand Tetons, a Utah

unimaginably ghostly and austere.

3.

Where do we go from here, across
what invincible knapweed, symbiotic
crush of foot and arrowhead

forming the spine
of a riverbed?


4.

One drops down into two,
wayward, ineffectual.

The vast heaven above dissolves
in its acutest angles and unsafe
cliffs, as a hawk cries
from a branch at the moment a poet is about to breach

that membrane between
ligament and ether, draft
and stillness of air blossoming

where geranium meets nitrogen:


5.

love!  What advances
away

from fingertips,
a silt

disengaging
root and mortar,

enveloping
logic like water,

whereupon one comes back
to the flesh,
metaphor

driven
to speak of a last light cascading
down the veins

of confederate rose mallow,
its pinkish, silk-thin blossom lasting
the duration
of one revolution
of the sun around the earth.

6.

You, of fish
and cataracts, a buoy
so far from the shoreline,

of sand
tracing the girth
of land with your feet,

of mountains
settling on your shoulders
to weigh the sun.

To keep the surf at bay
I hold your voice
in a crab's pincer-eyes,

waiting for the moon
to eclipse itself.  Thereby
joy becomes its own becoming.

7.

Montana, dry and wide
in August, leaning
with scythes.

Cloud speckles Utah's buttes
midafternoon.  Going down
to Yellowstone River,

a breeze lifts my arms,
the barest rippling
of a current

where my palms meet
water, where my feet
electrocute sand.


8.

October light hums
in my veins.

A freight train lumbers by
in a valley's pass,

carrying ore
to foundries, river ports.

This country
in my heart

wheels with a sun's
needling grass,

driving penstemon
into brief blue

encompassings! —

turning to mountains
throwing shade

across your brow.

# Picnic at Agua Caliente Canyon

1.

a touch
of salt on the back edges
of white birch

leaves drifts down
into the shade
of you lying back

on rock, a lunch
of dolmas and salmon
sushi at your fingertips,

a breeze crinkling
the net of veins that links
granite to birch-root,

as though you
were the furthest stem
of something coming

to completion:
a lizard's inertia breaking
into flight, a hoarse

canyon's whispering heat,
the leaping forward
of each moment's breath

from rock to rock.
what of this salt
so fleeting i can barely

trace its winding down
into fingerprints,
spiraling gradients

of cliff-faces?
time to go back.
love's time-piece ticking.


2.


to stand like a heart!
to drift like auroras!
to pierce the shape

of sunlight against
a cheekbone!  to stay
such grace of diameter

between helix and hair
of nape!  with what
do i measure

the angle of your knee
to the height of your gaze?
*tick. tick. tick.*


3.


what friend doesn't lie
in a lover's heart?
what petal could ever

really claim
its part in flowering
if not for the stickiness

of the pollen within?
to lie back in the face
of the sun is to claim

the work of the heart.
when two hearts close in
on each other

there is no contrivance
beyond friend:  it's
the song of its depth,

the clarity of its immolation,
its phoenix crest,
its horizon rowing

with the long blades
of crow-wings
away from what

defines
grey light breaking
into rainbow,

where cloud carries sky.
if later, no friend,
there never was friend.

therefore sky
listens to wind,
who merely

traces the salt
of your spine, my spine,
to find

an ocean's source
in the quiet of two hearts
flowering into a tree.

# IV

## Night Bloomers

*Cereus greggii*
blooms a delicate lunar white
in the midseason of my life.

Am I
to undertake another shovelful
of compost, a skull's

planter, a tangling vine
roping itself around
my spine,

while seizing
air in my hands
with the grip of one

in a cactus field grazing
for thorns
as sweet as thyme?

What drifts with the moon
along a street in the afternoon,
like a mime

I have no alphabet
for, neither sacred
nor profane?  Meanwhile, let's bet

on dust to lift their beds
from what careens
and averts,

while I take a walk at dusk with my shirt's
sleeves waving with prayers
and an epic poem's breath,

let go of what pristine
evanescent air
this cactus breathes,

its thin arms weaving
among themselves to bind
themselves, each to each, engraving

shadow with light.
There's nothing left to find
in the morning, when this cactus'

pollen vanishes with the stars.
Its petals are sharp,
so beautifully white,

giving themselves to countless deaths.

# A Night of Flamenco in Tel Aviv

A taxi
to Yahud Lamed Paretz #3 opens
its door in Tel Aviv to whisk me
off to a performance

of flamenco,
that Castilian dance so full of fire
in its rhapsodic lament I feel a slow
incandescent burn, a high-wire

of heels meeting stage,
as though all these human bodies gathered
to witness grace and electricity merged
were what we all shared,

however much one might
despair in solitude,
however much this basement theatre grows bright
with sorrow in its Hebrew

declensions, its lines
breaking down the backs
of Arabic script, an Islamic grain
in this air of heels making tracks

across this land of martyrs,
heretics, and holy sites.
We visit the Makhtesh Ramon crater
in the south, below the flight

patterns of F-16s, taking in
a view as vast
as erosion itself, the skin
of the ibex surmounting the crest

of its rim, its heart's shape
bordering the Negev Mountains,
the shape of Israel like the steep
stem of high heels, its plains

broiling with a sun fierce
with camels and Bedouins.
Water is scarce
here.  Atlantic pistachio trees define

a passage for spice and Roman armies.
Is there a difference
between now and then, a frieze
to depict a violence

as common as valor, as a high wind?
Rockets and suicide bombers have replaced
regiments of conquerors, a grand
advancement across a desert waste.

In this the dance of the flamenco,
how its rhythm knows a Palestinian grief,
how borders everywhere have always been sown
in blood, how I face the brief

glare of a girl-soldier on a train
to Haifa, a hatred brimming with the salt of a wound,
painting the terrain
a color of bone, my Buddhist robe maroon

and fringed with black and white
the source of her disdain,
and all I can think is, What fight
awaits her, on what stone

terrace etched with metaphor and a Mediterranean bay?
Has a Nazi's hate been transferred?
In this the dance of the Flamenco, how it stays
the hand of its audience with less than a word,

its wheeling sorrow dissolving borders,
its sweat risen from blood and the axles
of peasants and doctors and merchants alike bearing
away their heirlooms and gold, their scrolls

lettered with an ancestry from the same tree,
this road called *Al Nakba*, this road we all
must take if we're  to see
how commonplace our fall

not from Grace but from an ordinary
cause:  that of olive trees slightly leaning
with its harvest toward a Mediterranean Sea,
of a beach careening

into railroad tracks,
of a dance called the Flamenco,
its floor shaking
with artillery.  Long ago,

this crater had been a river that once had flowed
through a Sinai delta, when the world
had swayed as one Invincible God,
and the Flamenco was a flag never to be unfurled.

# "The Hanging Gardens" Perform

1.

After hooks in skin and lifting up
of bodies to a warehouse ceiling, epidermal
tents pitched to evoke
Frankenstein's veins,

a trio
of them in unflinching meditation,
in a limelight gone to the deepend
of queasy,

a freight train barrels past, a smorgasbord
of boxcars stuffed with delicatessen
factory hors' doeuvres,

gangland graffiti flickering by in big loops and
clanging curves.

Like yeah, brotherman.
Like shit, this beautiful Native American woman says

in back of a Camry luxury car she
wants the same hooks to hang
from her flesh, she so beautiful
of this earth and its pain I wonder
if this is how she came to be called
Spike — cables attached

to cloud perhaps.
She's more than a little drunk.
She's twenty, a mother, with this broad face.

Then it floods in me, the grasslands
that once sprawled
across Sonoran desert,
and I look down

at my hands, these careful
digits of mine,

after touching
the tornado inside a freight's entropy,
its caboose whispering
past bodies.

Should I say I love you
what would it be
to the crow nesting in your apple tree?

Would barbs of cholla and saguaro and ocotillo coalesce
into mountain peaks,

a human sentience,
a network of carotid arteries spanning a city?

2.

Who is this Yaqui mother
angling off
into a train's
midnight circumference?

She must cry out in her sleep
for her child
somewhere in Texas.

She must live in
a wind like the sun.
Can we say

what chant encapsulates,
sings, hums, corroborates

blood of you with blood of me,

lattices of dust and sunlight
with a momentum's heft of breath,

a gathering of alveoli
with touch of chrysanthemum?

These bodies dig their gardens
to irrigate
such a face,
its rows riven
by a locomotive's wheels.


3.

Days skitter by like leaves.

Out for a walk, sitting down
at a bus stop, my flesh coheres
around bone

to measure
the arc of falling bodies,
air gravitating to mouths opening to silence.

*Entropy.  Driftwood.  Cavern.*

A bus rolls by, huffing
its exhaust, as

twilight shrouds the hawk perched
on a powerline and
eating a mouse, an electric buzz drifting
over stucco roofs…

Why, yes! I say
to a hush of space
unraveling
into all who've come before,
a rising of water

into an aquifer
of graves.

## Simile Is Not Like Simile

Showed up at the poetry reading with my bottle
of crystal water and prayer wheel hooked
to my belt and there
was Charles Bernstein cadencing

his six-pence verse

with the sweet, unapologetic rhythm of a train's
shrieking pentameter.  At first

glance, the world's gone awry in the slyest
of its corners, simile
dying

between the lines
and alleyways of whatever marketplace,
wherever a poem's hinge
creaks with rust.

Yes, can't accuse Charles Bernstein of that one.

He rants like an angel —
assuming, of course, such celestial
creatures, quite soluble

in the path of their usual ascent,
manage to at least clear their throats

before going up onto stage — and, yes
what is that but a series of planks
hammered together with nails
once simple rock in the earth,
these days a forgotten element,

a slipshod trace of itself
in strata and stratospheres —
whereupon the listener, myself, consciously reflects
on the exact posture of his body (my own) as it presupposes (as I do) as he

(the poet from New York, bespectacled and fastidious

in his delivery)—no, there's no pre-
about it—that's exactly it! how to disregard
the bouncing back of one's focus
onto oneself, to be, rather,
symbiotically charged with the nether-

world of *this, this, this*...

*This* is like *this*, yes.
But what is really meant by that?

Later that night, I'm at a party, and there's
Charles Bernstein telling

me where the wine
is and I wander
about trying to find
a conversation, as happy
as I've ever been, when

it occurs to me
*like*
is a simile for *like*, as much to say

I liken
this sunset right now to no metaphor

at all,
especially
in how it
touches the deepest shadow my arms

throw,

blooms
gossamer
for the definite steel of the trains
punctuating C.'s poems—
which brings me back

to what seems to be the point
this side of the tracks and its hooting
parlance:

what is is is
presupposes any wish
to be anywhere else.

## The Holy Land

Black leather dress shoes sink into
the sands of the Mediterranean,

my suitcase somewhere
in Toronto, the Sheraton

Tel Aviv a glistening needle
in the eye of a country of camels

over my shoulder,
a pair of Israeli soldiers

in their bathing-suits batting
a rubber ball with wooden mallets

back and forth, its arc
cutting across a sun's circuit.

I ponder the possibility
of a Guinness at the Irish pub

on Rehov Mendeli
along the beach in Tel Aviv,

pull out twelve shekels for an umbrella
and a chair, while another wants to sell

me an ice cream on a stick—
another six.

An ocean brims with a holocaust
of tuna lost

to overzealous fishermen, an appetite
like a Great White's

for anything with fins
and a propensity for Corinthians,

this Biblical landscape
grown steep

with automobiles and bloodbaths,
a winding avenue of varying faiths

drifting into view.
What does it come down to?

A cocktail
at the local

open air eatery mirrors
a battery of cluster

bombs about to fall
on Beirut, while a trawler

in the distance inches
across a map pinched

by borders, creased
with troop divisions in a Middle East

fraught with mullahs and sheiks
devising ways to stake

out their claims
to holiness, a folk hero's fame

in Jordan and Egypt
having eclipsed

one named Bin Laden.
But right now I lean

back in my chair to see
what sophistry

a Mediterranean surf
might offer

me in its iambic
curling back

upon itself, if actual words
can be heard

in its detonations,
as though to say it wonders when

Israelis and the Lebanese
will dare to suffer peace

among themselves.
Words are open graves

in either lexicon.
Blood is holy even

when it spills.
And children

are lifted out of fallen buildings
while Boeing is gilding

its tax havens with a windfall
not seen since the Nazis threw all

those American Union
Banking Corporation millions

into weapons, leaflets.
But right now I get

up from my chair and make
my way back

to #14 Mendeli,
after stopping at a deli

for an eggplant casserole,
some green beans, a roll

loaded with butter and sesame seeds.
Hatred matches hatred.

Hezbollah rockets streak into Haifa.
Grief matches grief.

But right now I look out
across a sleeping city,

its mortar volcanic,
its citizenry safely behind brick

and dreaming of a boundless field
they all stand in, with hands folded

behind them, looking up to a sun
bursting to finally break open.

# A Reading at a Bookstore in Bozeman, Montana


Full of a bright hunger
for what holds
and collapses away

from my hands,
I grab a shovel and dig,
an entire alphabet hovering
between what is to be seen
and what mind
envelops, a shifting

menagerie of awnings,
portcullises,
hanging ladders,
steep rooves,

throwing my shoulders
into caliché, its unraveling

knots, mind veering
away to the arc of a September sun,
a vista red salvia touching
its aureole after
finding earth.

The morning light plays down my arms like rainwater,
the clouds of a sudden monsoon
breaching

the loudness, the impervious sound, the collision
of all things coming together
in a red flower breaking free
of its root and spiraling
straight into the sun,

a windowsill growing a hummingbird's wings,

a Red Bird of Paradise submitting
its tiny slender leaves
to the albino caterpillar hooking

its hind-end to sudden sunlight
while tea of the ginseng root brews
in half-

light.  It suddenly comes
back to me the memory
of the one person

who showed up at my reading in Bozeman, Montana,
a geologist, perhaps a lover
of red rock along dark roads,

and how the whole world opened
up like a beautiful
woman then.

That next day I stare
straight ahead,

a laggard horse, tan-spotted, lumbering
out of a Montana corral,
into a road bordered by a skyline,

the hills rolling away with the fervency
of a last kiss.

I dream myself under a limber pine
by a pond full of river trout,
cows wandering like sadhus.

It breaks free, desire.
It enters into the petals
of weeds, a horse's

yellowing grass,

as I come back
to the desert,
its living vein
of truth,

its burrowing mountains, its rainbow
that cannot be seen.

I dream of a car that fails
on an open highway,
of one who paints
on his ass a blurred self-portrait

of Jesus Christ, or the
Virgin Mary, or Saint Therese,

of suns that cast
the shadows of their profiles
into the shapes of canyons and craters alike,

of bitter acacias shadowing
the swallowing descent of rare butterflies,

a door opening to white
persimmon rising —

all this happening
in some other world,

my hands growing into red rock,
a waking pain
so full of God

I breathe the dusk-
light the way a moth
grazes oleander,

my olive tree
within.

T. Luis Cox is the author of an epic poem on the life of the great Buddhist master Padmasambhava called "The Lotus King." He teaches writing at the Tohono O'odham Community College on the tribal reservation near Sells, Arizona, and directs the Tibetan Meditation Center of Tucson. Born in Toquepala, Peru, he lived in California, Indiana and Ohio before moving to Tucson, Arizona in 1987 to mentor under Steve Orlen through the M.F.A. program in creative writing at the University of Arizona.

www.ingramcontent.com/pod-product-compliance
Lightning Source LLC
Chambersburg PA
CBHW081339090426
42737CB00017B/3218